10/14

D1401358

SHARE!
PRESENT YOUR FINDINGS

Emma Carlson Berne

PowerKiDS press.

Published in 2015 by The Rosen Publishing Group, Inc.
29 East 21st Street, New York, NY 10010

First Edition

Editor: Jennifer Way
Book Design: Kate Vlachos
Photo Research: Katie Stryker

Photo Credits: Cover, p. 14 Blend Images/Ariel Skelley/the Agency Collection/Getty Images; p. 5 kkgas/E+/Getty Images; p. 6 Rob Marmion/Shutterstock; p. 7 Valueline/Thinkstock; p. 9 Jupiterimages/Brand X Pictures/Thinkstock; pp. 10, 13, 16 (right) iStockphoto/Thinkstock; p. 11 Thinkstock Images/Comstock/Thinkstock; p. 12 Adam Haglund/Maskot/Getty Images; p. 15 Fuse/Thinkstock; p. 16 (left) Monashee Frantz/OJO Images/Getty Images; p. 17 Charles D Winters/Photo Researchers/Getty Images; p. 18 Brand X Pictures/Thinkstock; p. 19 Bec Parsons/Lifesize/Getty Images; p. 20 Izabela Habur/E+/Getty Images; p. 21 Wavebreak Media/Thinkstock; p. 22 Source - Science/Photo Researchers/Getty Images.

Library of Congress Cataloging-in-Publication Data

Berne, Emma Carlson, author.
  Share! : present your findings / by Emma Carlson Berne. — First edition.
    pages cm. — (The scientific method in action)
Includes index.
ISBN 978-1-4777-2931-1 (library) — ISBN 978-1-4777-3018-8 (pbk.) — ISBN 978-1-4777-3089-8 (6-pack)
1. Science–Methodology—Juvenile literature. 2. Research—Juvenile literature. 3. Science—Experiments—Juvenile literature. I. Title.
Q175.2.B4745 2015
507.2′1—dc23
                                    2013027103

Manufactured in the United States of America

CPSIA Compliance Information: Batch #WS14PK5: For Further Information contact Rosen Publishing, New York, New York at 1-800-237-9932

CONTENTS

Sharing with Others 4

The Last Step 6

Prepare to Share 8

Writing a Report 10

Making Graphic Organizers 12

Making Models and Displays 14

Giving a Presentation 16

Science Fairs 18

Scientists Share, Too! 20

Building Knowledge Through Collaboration 22

Glossary 23

Index 24

Websites 24

SHARING WITH OTHERS

Imagine that you have made scientific **observations** and asked questions. Then you formulated a **hypothesis**. After that, you planned, conducted, and completed an **experiment**. Next, you analyzed the **data** from your experiment and determined whether or not your hypothesis was correct. Do you think you have completed all the steps in the **scientific method**?

You're not done yet! The very last step in the scientific method is sharing your results with others. In the following chapters, you will learn about the different ways you can share your results with your teacher and other students.

The observations and notes you take during an experiment help you analyze your results. They also give you the information you need to prepare reports and share your findings.

THE LAST STEP

Sharing your results is a way of teaching others what you have learned.

When you think of someone sharing the results of an experiment, you might picture a white-coated scientist. She stands in front of an audience of hundreds, reading from a paper about the latest, cutting-edge scientific discoveries.

That is not exactly what you will do when you share the results of your experiment with your class.

You will use the scientific method when you do a science project, though. After you have answered scientific questions through performing experiments, it is important that you share your results. Scientific discoveries, even ones made by kids, need to be shared so that others can learn from them.

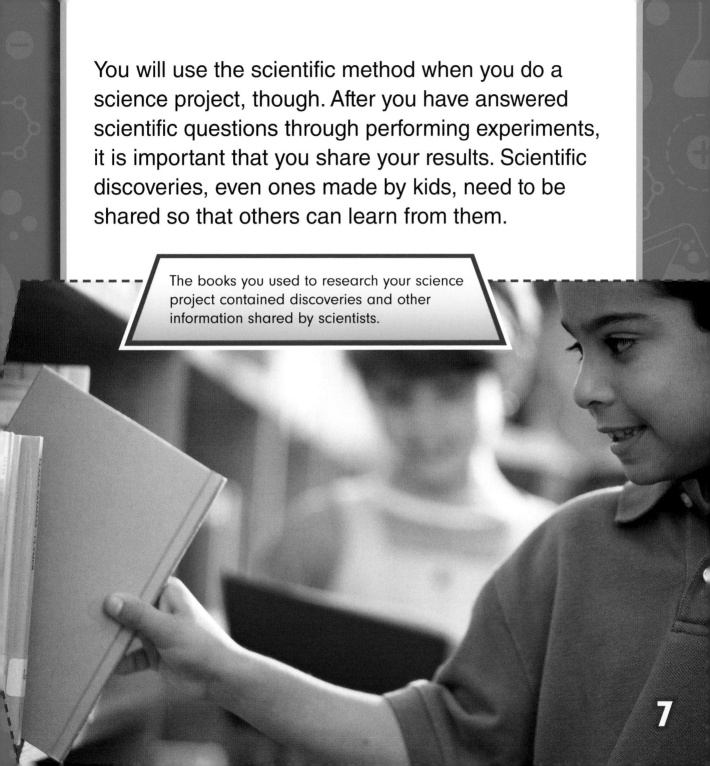

The books you used to research your science project contained discoveries and other information shared by scientists.

PREPARE TO SHARE

The way you choose to share your results depends on what type of experiment you did and where you plan to share your results. Sometimes you might only need to write up your results in a report. This format will work best if your experiment was an assignment to be handed in to the teacher.

Sometimes you are expected to present your findings to your teacher, your class, or at a **science fair**. To do this, you could create a digital slideshow or make a large poster or models for display. You can also write a speech or create a simple website that explains your results.

> Write up clear notes that explain your hypothesis and experiment and that contain your data and results. Then you can use those notes to create the parts of your presentation.

WRITING A REPORT

Explaining everything that happened in your experiment in your report helps others understand how you got your results.

No matter how you will be sharing your results, you will still want to write up a report. A report is a written summary of your experiment and results.

The report will walk readers through the process of your project, in order of the scientific method. First, present your initial hypothesis and your observations.

A librarian can teach you how to use computer programs to write your report or create parts of your presentation.

Then, explain how and why you designed your experiment, and tell the reader how you ran the experiment. Then, present your analyzed data. Finally, discuss whether your hypothesis was proven or disproven and talk about any plans for future experiments.

SCIENCE TIPS

You can also share your findings in the form of a website. You can ask a teacher to show you how to do this.

MAKING GRAPHIC ORGANIZERS

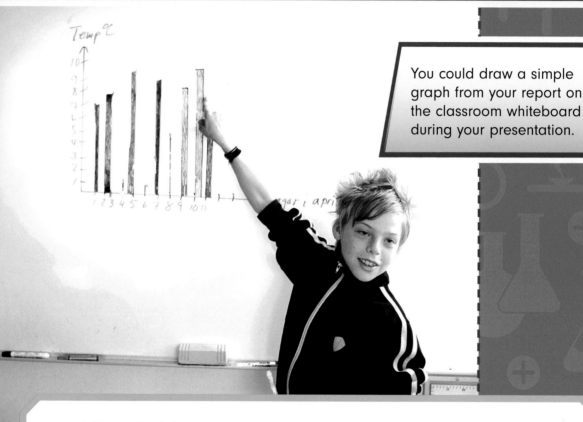

You could draw a simple graph from your report on the classroom whiteboard during your presentation.

Visual aids help people understand your findings more easily. Whether you are writing a report, making a website, or presenting at a science fair, you will want to include **graphic organizers**, such as charts and graphs.

Charts are great for listing many numbers or measurements in an orderly way. Graphs can help your audience understand the patterns you already identified and explained in your report. You can draw your charts or graphs with markers on big sheets of poster board, or you can create your graphic organizers on the computer. Computer-drawn charts and graphs are often neater and easier to read than hand-drawn ones.

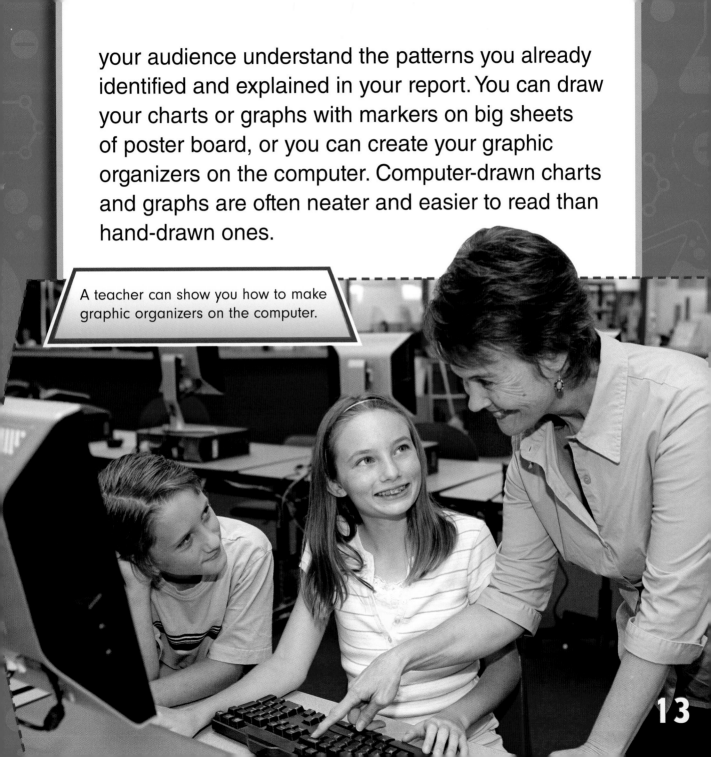

A teacher can show you how to make graphic organizers on the computer.

MAKING MODELS AND DISPLAYS

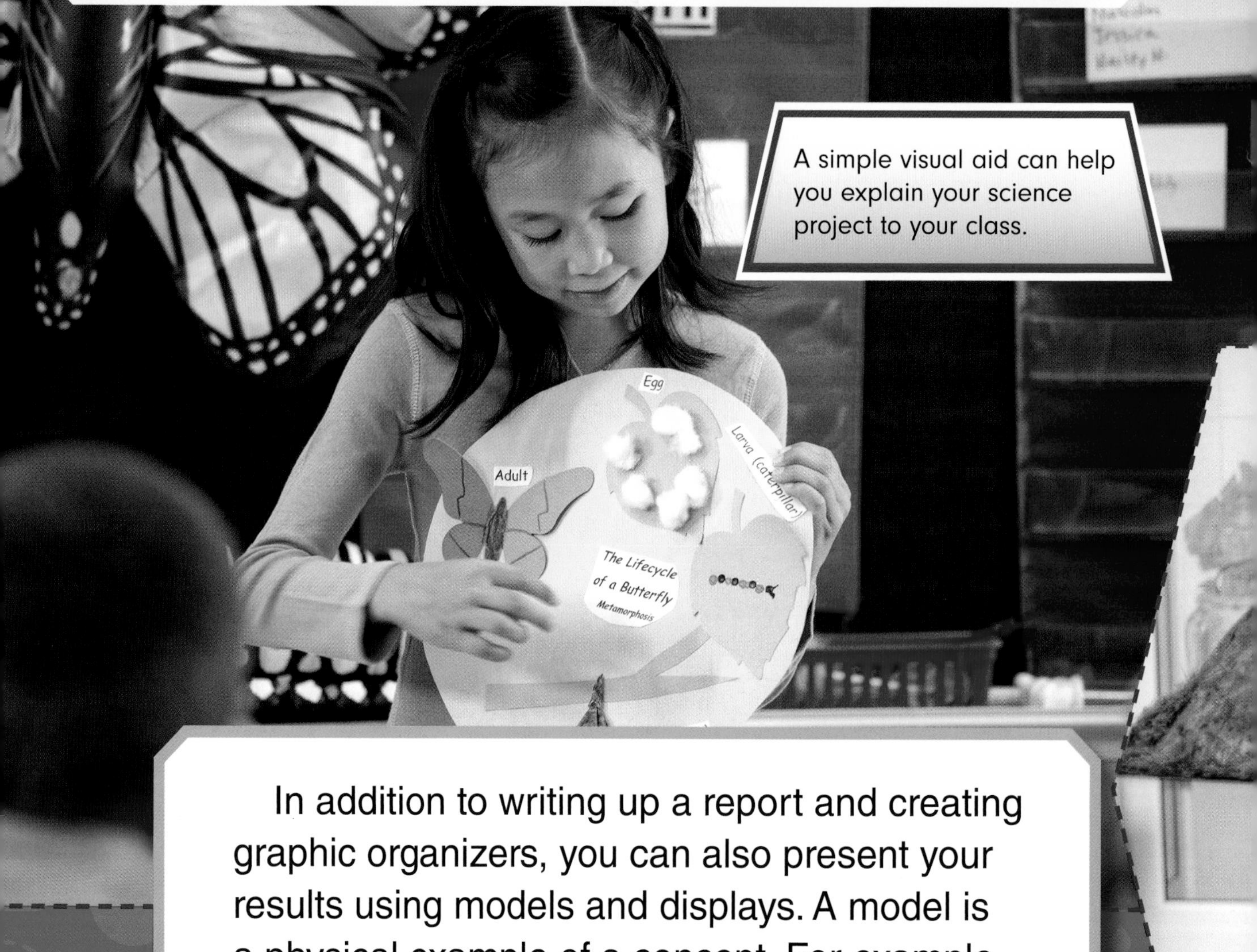

A simple visual aid can help you explain your science project to your class.

Egg

Larva (caterpillar)

Adult

The Lifecycle of a Butterfly

Metamorphosis

In addition to writing up a report and creating graphic organizers, you can also present your results using models and displays. A model is a physical example of a concept. For example, mixing baking soda and vinegar in a cone of clay is a model of how a volcano erupts.

As a display, consider bringing in portions of your experiment at different points. For example, if your experiment involves plant development, display photographs of your plants at different points of growth.

A model of a volcano is fun to make, and it helps you demonstrate how lava flows out of a volcano.

GIVING A PRESENTATION

Perhaps your teacher or the judges at a science fair have asked you to give an **oral presentation** about your project. To prepare for this, first write notes on index cards. You can study these notes before your oral presentation. You can also use them during your presentation

When you make notes, you do not need to write down everything you will say. Writing down your main points will help you feel confident about speaking in front of people.

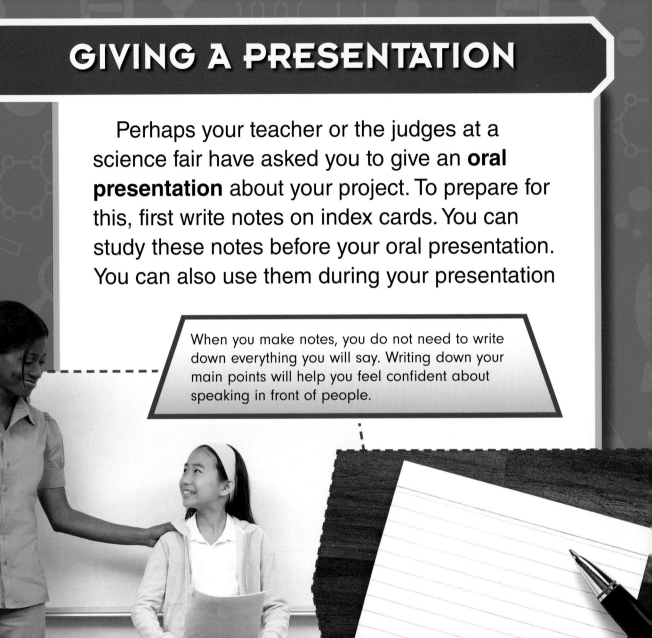

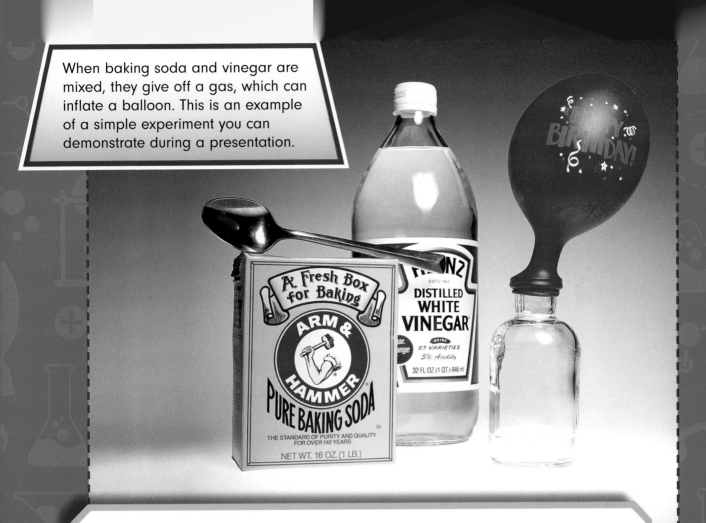

When baking soda and vinegar are mixed, they give off a gas, which can inflate a balloon. This is an example of a simple experiment you can demonstrate during a presentation.

to stay focused. You will also want to have visual aids to illustrate important points in your presentation.

You may find it scary to talk in front of a group. This is totally normal. Remember that your teacher or the science fair judges are eager to hear your presentation. You're in front of a friendly audience!

SCIENCE FAIRS

Your science fair display can include a combination of posters with graphic organizers, models, and a demonstration of your experiment.

A science fair is one of the most fun places to share your scientific **conclusions**. If you participate in a science fair, you will be expected to have a model, display, or presentation about your experiment. You should also bring multiple copies of your written report to hand out.

You and the other students will arrange your displays on tables. Parents, judges, and teachers walk around and look at the different presentations. Once the judges stop at your table, they will want to hear an oral presentation about your findings and possibly see a demonstration. Then they might give you a grade or even award you a prize!

If your experiment has ongoing results, such as growing plants, you can bring them in to display at the science fair.

SCIENTISTS SHARE, TOO!

Scientists share their results in almost the same way as students. They write reports called papers, in which they explain their discoveries. These papers are published in scientific **journals**, which other scientists read. Scientists also share results on websites, blogs, or in radio or TV interviews.

A scientist might give a presentation called a lecture at a school or a library. There, he will talk about his research and his discoveries.

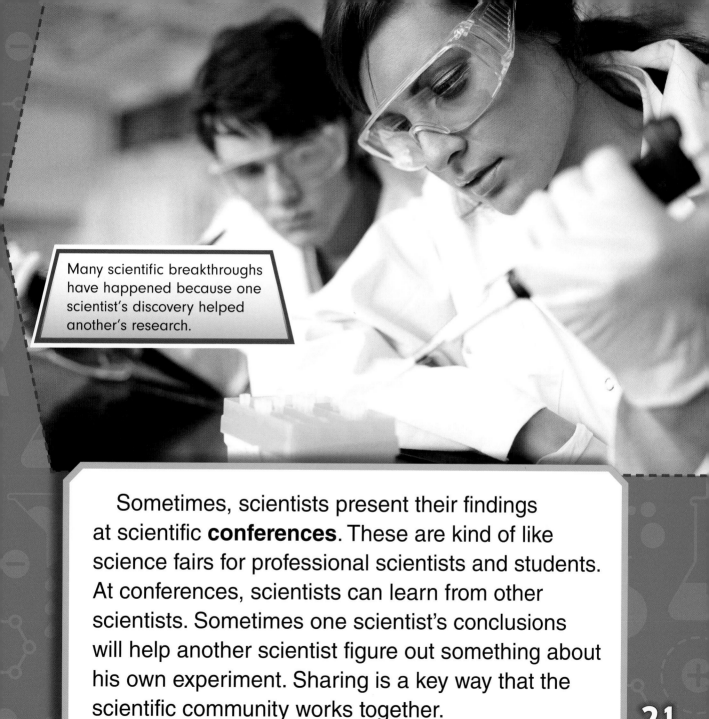

Many scientific breakthroughs have happened because one scientist's discovery helped another's research.

Sometimes, scientists present their findings at scientific **conferences**. These are kind of like science fairs for professional scientists and students. At conferences, scientists can learn from other scientists. Sometimes one scientist's conclusions will help another scientist figure out something about his own experiment. Sharing is a key way that the scientific community works together.

BUILDING KNOWLEDGE THROUGH COLLABORATION

Imagine a scientist working on the cure for a disease. She works for many years and, eventually, discovers something important about the disease. She shares her findings at a conference. Another scientist says he has been working on another part of the cure. He shares the results from his experiments. By sharing their results, these scientists can get closer to curing the disease.

This kind of **collaboration** can happen only when scientists share their results. This is important to building our scientific knowledge.

In 1951, James Watson (right) began collaborating with Francis Crick (left) on research Crick had been working on. Working together, these scientists made important discoveries in biology.

GLOSSARY

collaboration (kuh-la-buh-RAY-shun) A partnership in which people work jointly toward a common goal.

conclusions (kun-KLOO-zhunz) The judgments that can be made after studying results.

conferences (KON-feh-rents-ez) Meetings at which people who work in the same field share findings.

data (DAY-tuh) Facts.

experiment (ik-SPER-uh-ment) A test done on something to learn more about it.

graphic organizers (GRA-fik OR-guh-ny-zerz) Charts, graphs, and pictures that sort facts and ideas and make them clear.

hypothesis (hy-PAH-theh-ses) Something that is suggested to be true for the purpose of an experiment or argument.

journals (JER-nulz) Magazines that present information about a subject, such as law or medicine.

observations (ahb-ser-VAY-shunz) Things that are seen or noticed.

oral presentation (OR-ul prih-zen-TAY-shun) A spoken report.

science fair (SY-unts FAYR) An event at which students present science projects, which are judged and graded.

scientific method (sy-en-TIH-fik MEH-thud) The system of running experiments in science.

INDEX

C
class, 6, 8
conclusions, 18, 21
conference(s),
    21–22

D
data, 4, 11
discoveries, 6–7, 20

E
experiment(s), 4,
    6–8, 10–11, 15,
    18, 21–22

F
format, 8

H
hypothesis, 4, 10–11

J
journals, 20

O
observations, 4, 10

P
paper(s), 6, 20

Q
questions, 4, 7

R
report, 8, 10, 12–14,
    18, 20
results, 4, 6–8, 10,
    14, 20, 22

S
science project, 7
scientist(s), 6, 20–22
slideshow, 8
students, 4, 19–21

WEBSITES

Due to the changing nature of Internet links, PowerKids Press has developed an online list of websites related to the subject of this book. This site is updated regularly. Please use this link to access the list:
www.powerkidslinks.com/smia/share/

24